THE BED

Jacques Tutcher   Selima Hill

Fair Acre Press

First published in Great Britain in 2024 by Fair Acre Press www.fairacrepress.co.uk

A CIP catalogue record for this book is available from
the British Library

ISBN 978-1-911048-78-7

Cover photograph Jacques Tutcher © 2024

*Special thanks to Sonia, Rod and Nicola
at the Black Dog Tea Room in Lyme Regis
for giving us space for our chats,
and for supplying us with excellent tea and cakes.*

*And thank you, Tom and Hayley and all the team
at Amid Giants and Idols for
your warmth and hospitality (except on Mondays!)*

For Alison

from Selima, and your brother Jacques

Jacques Tutcher

Earthman wanderer; child of nature.
Mostly self taught and making it up along the way, currently studying
Photography at Falmouth University.
I like pictures and words that unfold through my lens.
It's my processing practice, travelling never arriving.

Selima Hill

Selima Hill is a pilot and a paramedic and
breeds pot-bellied pigs. In her dreams.

Contents

Every single movement, every thought is watching itself, each emotion starts but never finishes, and finally even the object of your longing becomes artificial and unreal. Only the longing is real, imposing conditions on you - that you must have something you don't possess, or touch someone who doesn't exist.

from Olga Tokarczuk's House of Day, House of Night
Translated by Antonia Lloyd-Jones

What Happens If He's Ill

What happens if he's ill?
Well, he *is* ill!
Do I get to see him?
I do not.
Will he get better?
No one knows.
Will I always love him?
I will.

Bedtime

I have been entrusted to a spider.
I put my tiny arms round his neck.

I sleep beside him in his dusty nook
and as I fall asleep

I hear the spider
tell me stories in a voice like thread.

Everything That Happened at the Lake

Everything that happened at the lake –
the stillness of the water, the accident,
how he was transported by grief –
is happening again and again

but every day it happens further off
until today I can barely hear
the crunches of his footsteps on the gravel
on their way to somewhere I can't see.

A Spider in a Dressing-Gown

He needs me like a spider needs a dressing-gown:
the only thing I do is weigh him down –

and how can he be happy, *weighed down*?
How can he untangle himself?

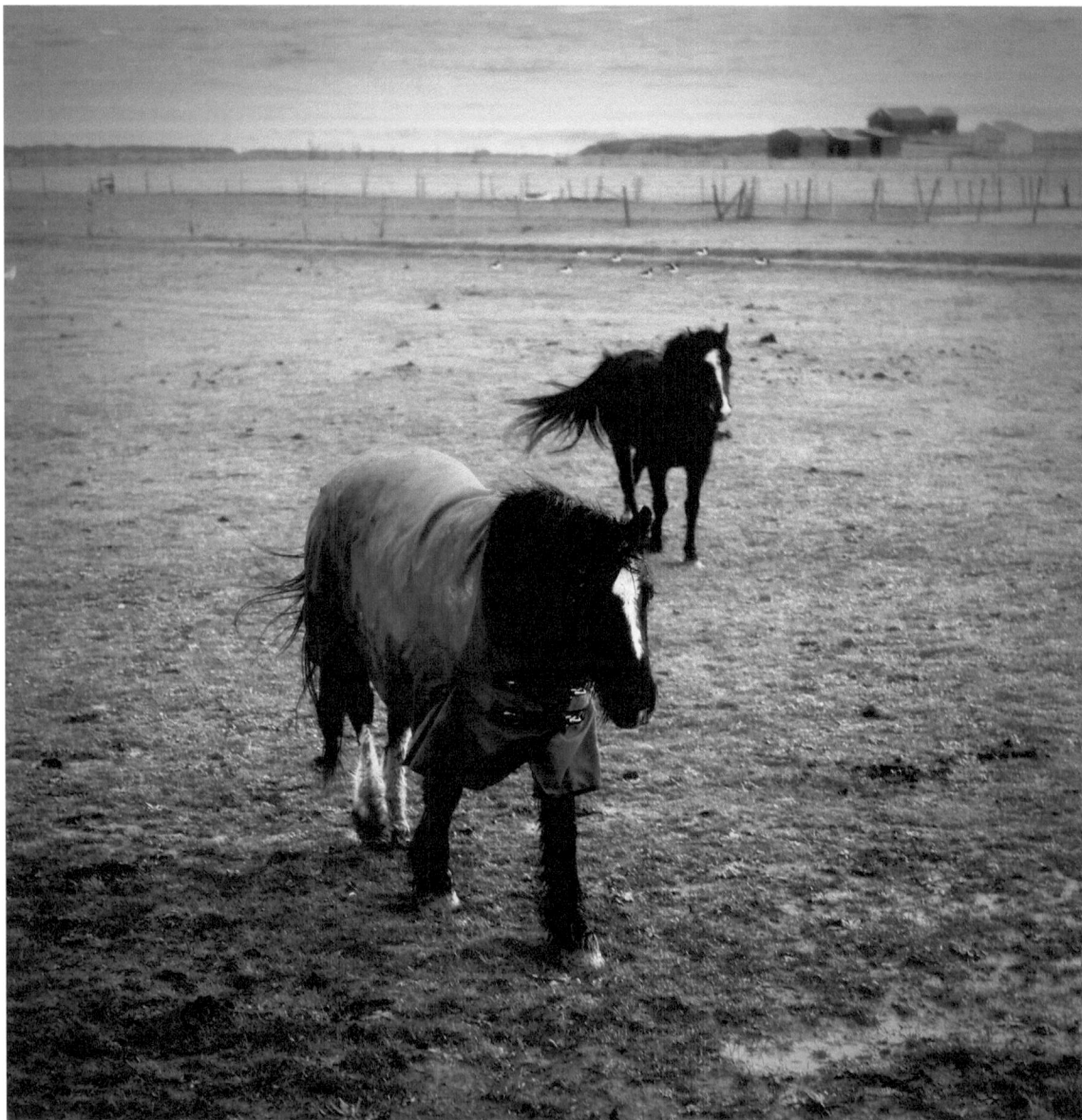

The Dancer

I prayed to God for a six-foot spider
or, if that can't be done, a six-foot man –

and there he was, a man I seemed to know
and yet I'd never seen him before.

Hiding in the Airing-Cupboard

I used to like to hide in the airing-cupboard –
constricting, yes, but in a safe way:

I heard my friends and family come and go
but far away, as I now hear T.

Hope

Honestly I don't need to know
where he lives or anything like that –

I just need to know *how to worry*,
if to hope he's happy is to worry.

Hyacinths

Other people call, and send him cards,
and ask him how he is, and bring him hyacinths –

other people who would be completely mystified,
as I am, by the way I find I envy them.

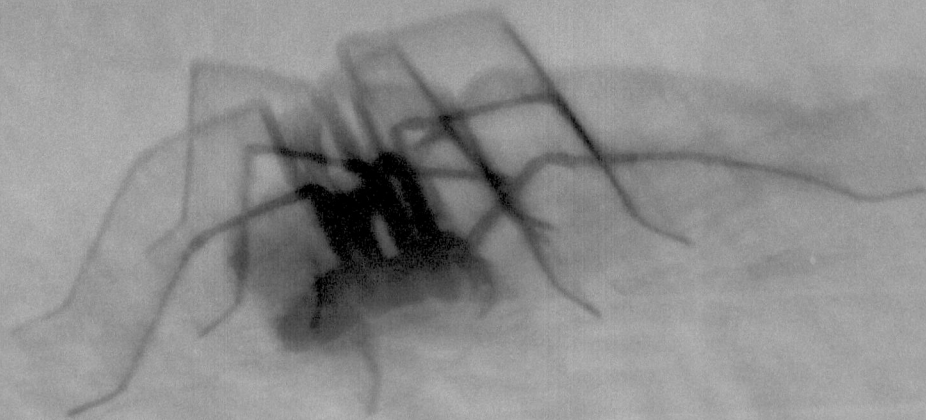

Please Can I Confide in You

Please can I confide in you, the reader.
I'm trying to be honest.   But it's hard.

It's hard to be both honest and not hurtful.
And hurting him would be unforgivable.

Spiderlings

I need to not have known him.   It was pointless.
The dream of fish that dream of warm hair.

I need to dream of something else.   And T.
needs to be kept warm and dry

like spiderlings to whom I need to whisper
I'm sorry.

One Sunny Day

One sunny day a spider appeared
and then, without a word, he disappeared,

leaving behind him an absence
completely different

from the peaceful absence
in the house before the spider came.

The Accident

Yes, it is his birthday today
but no, I must not send him a card:

I need to not exist.   And the accident
needs to never have existed either.

The Dog Who Whines

I know a dog who trots into the garden
then runs and runs round and round the house

until she finds a door that isn't open
and here she sits and whines to be let in.

The Offering

Please can someone take me outside
and pour a bucket of water over my head.

Please can someone wrap their arms around me
and squeeze me till I beg them to stop.

Please can someone go to his house
and offer him a tray of chocolate mousses.

Another Day in Hell

Ever since the day I met the man
with legs like pampas grass and bony hands

that fly like whippets flying after rats,
every day's another day in Hell.

The Spider Hotel

Wrap me, wrap me, spiders of the world,
wrap me in your swathing bands and squeeze me,

I don't mind a bit, I'm breeding flies
just for you, I have prepared dark nooks

for you to come and hide in and relax in,
and practise your ballooning from, and weaving in;

entangle me, spiders of the world;
grip me gently – like my dreams of T.

Dreams of T.?   What dreams of T.?   The dreams
I don't know how to stop myself from dreaming.

The Stranger

A man appears
and then disappears,

leaving me to re-befriend
my mouse.

Feeling Sad is Such a Waste of Time

Feeling sad is such a waste of time –
duckweed, pondweed, mermaids in aquaria,
sunspots, gunshots, cocktail sausages;
beanpoles, flagpoles, towpaths, eucalypti;
vanity; iniquity; the heartlessness
of certain kleptoparasitic spiders;
slobwear, concrete, luxury hotels,
his tolerance, his smile, chocolate mousses,
lemon mousses – all a waste of time.

The Track to the Lake

When I pass the track to the lake –
usually with people who don't know him,
after all it's nearly two years now –

every time I pass I think of T.
I'm like a fly entangled in his legs,
his two long legs like two long lengths of loneliness

if loneliness was made of long bones.
I tell myself I *mustn't* and I *won't* –
but when I pass the track I think of T.

Visiting Hours

Although I long to visit him in hospital
I may be stupid but I'm not that stupid.

There are other people in his life
to visit him and send him greeting cards:

nurses, priests and loved ones are expected
to stand beside his bed but not me.

Please Can I Have a Lake

Please can I have a lake
in which to skinny-dip;

to wave to people having picnics from;
to float along upside-down in silence on;

a lake to love,
to drown my sorrows in.

Ward 2

Unfortunately feeling sad is boring.
I think about nothing but myself.

I think I'm feeling sad because of him
but actually it's all about *myself*.

I think about nothing but *myself*.
Feeling sad is just a waste of time.

Get Well Soon

Pictures of guitars and boats and roses,
grazing horses, golfers, snow-capped peaks,

pink flamingos, someone's sausage-dog,
a nifty yellow sports car, more roses.

What It Is He Wants

Day by day the real T. recedes
and another T. takes his place,

an even thinner T., who no one sees,
who wanders in and out as if he owns the place –

like a saint appearing in a chapel,
the way you never know when he'll be there –

and if I ask him what it is he wants
he doesn't even bother to reply.